Tai Chi for Beginners

*The Ultimate Guide to Supercharge Your Mind,
Increase Your Energy & Feel Amazing By Unlocking
the Power of Tai Chi*

Table of Contents

Introduction

First and foremost I want to thank you for downloading the book, "Tai Chi for Beginners: The Ultimate Guide to Supercharge Your Mind, Increase Your Energy & Feel Amazing By Unlocking the Power of Tai Chi".

In this book you will learn how to achieve harmony of your inner and outer self by integrating your mind and body by practicing the ancient Chinese martial art, Tai chi. Here, you will be introduced to a popular self-defense and calisthenics exercise, learn about its history, where it originated from, and how it flourished through the years, not only in the East but also in the Western world. With the aim to guide you in unleashing the power of Tai chi, you will learn the variations in style of this meditation art form and use its essential principles to a healthier, harmonious, and happy life.

This book lays down the important elements of this ancient Chinese tradition, its potential health benefits, and why it is a safe and effective complementary therapy to manage a wide range of medical conditions. Additionally, this book aims to teach you how Tai chi balances the mind, body, and spirit. You will also learn how to get started with this calming exercise, get tips on other important details you might overlook as a Tai chi beginner, from wearing the proper attire to choosing the right style that will appeal to you. You will also get to know the many types of weapons that you can use to hone your skills more. So, why not start your journey and unlock the power of

Tai chi? This simple, easy-to-read book is the key to making an ancient martial art a way of life you might want to embrace forever!

Thanks again for downloading this book, I hope you enjoy it!

Chapter 1: Tai Chi History: When, Where and Why?

People of today think of the martial arts as something that requires punching, fighting, and kicking. They are synonymous with combat and usually hail a winner in the end. But the essence of a martial art is self-discipline, physical health, and mental focus and flexibility. Tai chi is a Chinese martial art that has been practiced for centuries for its health benefits as well as for its uses in battle. It involves slow, meditative body movements which offer a calming and peaceful effect for the practitioner.

Since the 1980s, Tai chi has been a well-known term in the Western world. Its popularity has flourished as a graceful and controlled exercise that almost anybody can enjoy. Accurate as this perception is, no doubt borne from stirring images of expansive plazas in China filled with generations of locals preparing mind and body for the day ahead, little is known or understood about its origins. For many, Tai chi is a lifestyle choice. For most casual practitioners, it is a hugely beneficial method of maintaining physical health and wellbeing while experiencing some of its meditative and spiritual qualities that have endured since its origins.

But what actually is it? At its core, Tai chi is a deadly martial art. In trained hands, it is a devastating method of combat that has been used by warriors for centuries. Customary of many art-forms of its kind in the East, Tai chi mimics the movements of native animals; the sweeping motions can be compared to that of the crane and the snake. Tai chi also summons and channels the core energy central to Eastern belief systems called 'Qi' (pronounced 'chee'). Qi is the interaction of five elements: earth, water, metal, fire and wood. The Chinese believe that these elements interact within all living things, and achieving good balance between them in your own self is important for mental and physical health. Qi is the overall flow of this energy, and the main benefactor of several disciplinary practices, not least, tai chi.

Whether your goals are physical or spiritual; improvements in strength, posture, and flexibility of body or of mind, Tai chi is an excellent addition to any lifestyle and at any age.

Debate has long raged about the origins of Tai chi ch'uan (to give it its proper name – literally translated as 'the beginning of boxing/combat'). Many scholars believe the original art dates back over 2500 years, while some place its conception around the 6th century AD or even later. The uncertainty in its origin is owed to a lack of verifiable historical information and artifacts, and opinions and assumptions have been largely formed by modern day scholars by way of connecting philosophies of the various Chinese dynasties and belief systems. Connections between the Taoist and Buddhist monasteries of early China are often cited but bear little in the way of evidence.

Many believe, though, that the modern form of T'ai chi ch'uan can trace its roots to between 300 and 700 years ago, to an almost mythical Shaolin Monk by the name of Chang San-Feng, who gave up hard combat methods for a softer and more tactical approach, using internal energy and force as his main weapon. He is said to have used the battle between a snake and a crane as his inspiration. A crane, in theory, should have little trouble in killing a snake, but as the crane goes for the snake's head, the snake would evade the attack and whip the crane with its tail. These interpretations of nature's battles are thought to have founded the basic movements of Tai chi as a martial art, and are responsible for the flowing motions we now recognize.

It is without question, however, that devotees have been practicing for many centuries before the rest of the world became privileged to its existence. Though fantastical and almost mythological to the modern mindset, the uncertainties surrounding its origins do not present as a barrier of entry to most, but only serve to enhance its mystical qualities and perpetuate its endurance as an art-form that continues to thrive in the modern world.

Chapter 2: Tai Chi Styles and Forms

T'ai chi comes in many forms and styles, and beginners and newcomers often find it hard to choose which one might be best suited to them. It is important to note that the main differences that set them apart are the pace and speed as well as the body poses and movements.

There are 5 major styles of Tai chi, and each of them is named after the families that first introduced them.

Yang Style

Founded by Yang Lu Chan, who earned the nickname "Yang the Invincible" for his skills, Yang style is the most popular among the five and is popular the world over. If you see a bunch of people doing Tai chi in a park or in a public area, they are likely to be practicing the Yang style.

It is typically performed in slow, steady motions, helping practitioners relax and attain the optimum flow of energy. Many see its moves as lyrical because of its grace and emphasis on relaxation.

In its combatting form, it is not a rushing movement that releases a knockout blow; rather, the blow is more of a dance step.

Chen Style

The oldest form of Tai chi is the Chen style, which emphasizes fast transitions and coiling moves that involve stamping and releasing the power of Yang style in smooth actions. It appears to an observer as being extremely strong and physically demanding.

The Chen style's trademark is to perform as if one was reeling silk. Just think of the arduous task of untangling the cocoon of a silk worm using just a single thread. It requires the lightest touch and smooth and circular motions, accompanied by continuous pressure.

Sun Style

Created by Sun Lu-Tang, the Sun style is known for its flowing motions with unique footwork. Because of its gentle postures, it is considered as an ideal exercise for older people and a therapeutic martial art.

This style involves less punching and kicking and has a higher stance. The movements are almost of the same tempo, and with a strong emphasis on Qigong, making it preferable for the older participant.

Sun Style is often compared to the Chen style because of its similarities in terms of Tai chi principles. Both styles also share common grounds in the structure of the forms, movement execution, and benefits to self-defense capabilities and health.

Wu Style

Wu style involves a minor inclination of the body for many of its movements. It is based on the Yang style, but is more compact, requiring a smaller area of work than most others. An outsider might find this style a little boring to watch, with its slow and sometimes minute physical movements. However, it is on the inside where all the action takes place. The big movements and flow of energy happens in the interior of the body. Rather than in the movements of the arms and legs, the pressure is generated through the opening and closing of the joints.

In terms of self-defense, the Wu style constitutes moves and postures suitable for fighting. However, the steady flows are an equally effective way to reduce stress and attain the health benefits associated. To relieve tension, its deep internal stretches can go a long way. This is why it is ideal for those who are looking for a more quiet and meditative practice. Newcomers who have a desire to train their core and improve health in their joints and stabilizing muscles will find this style a very worthwhile pursuit.

Wu (Hao) Style

Considered 5th in terms of popularity is the Wu or Wu (Hao)-style, which was developed in China in the 19th century and was created by Wu Xu-Yiang. Most of the foot movements are extremely small; however, the hand positions are precise but with occasional full extensions of the outer extremities of the body.

Some of the characteristics of this style are its simple postures with complicated techniques, control of *qi*, coherence, and strict demands of the body and posture. The actions are simple, but are absolutely practical and with profound meanings. Regarding posture, the hip should be tucked in, shoulders loosened, and back straightened. This is to protect the crotch, control the mind, and allow the energy to travel through the *qi* reservoir. In this style, the movements need to be consistent, and broken links or any shortcomings should be avoided as much as possible.

Many forms of Tai chi styles use swords or other weapons, but there are those who believe that weapons are not a core part of Tai chi. If by chance weapons are used, they must be held loosely to ensure that the qi, an energy force that is believed to flow through the body, will reach the tips.

Energy, Body, Spirit of the Styles

Learning the art of Tai chi serves as a workout for the body and energy, and offers advancement in these areas like few other disciplines. Even if a practitioner opts out of its spiritual offerings, the form always begins with the body, leading to improved health and wellbeing.

Energy

The abilities of advanced Tai chi masters come from a variety of functional types of subtle energy. This energy is where practitioners can unlock the secrets of Tai chi, wherein they train for years just to fully master the art.

The increasing life-force energy has the ability to provide healing as well as the passage to advanced mental capacities. With constant practice, it is not difficult for a beginner to achieve so too. People who have erratic energy levels and sensitivity to disruption can find Tai chi helpful, as it helps ground and smoothen the energy, allowing them to manage their talents and abilities more effectively in their daily lives.

Body

The body is the vessel in which the spirit and energy flows. With the help of Tai chi, practitioners are able to command the body and lead it to divide the body down to its most delicate aspects. The way to achieve this is by understanding and learning its physical realities and mechanisms, including how body parts work in conjunction when performing both strenuous and everyday tasks.

Spirit

In Chinese tradition, the spirit is a treasure alongside the body and energy. It works within the mind of all of us. It is vital to apply the energy of the spirit to reach the root of oneself and to be able to release personal power, achieve inner peace, and engage mind potential.

The way to work the energy, body, and spirit is just like learning music. You need to understand the basic techniques so as to come up with the right blend and flow. In advanced stages of Tai chi, all of these elements should blend into one so as to attain the greatness of this martial art form.

Chapter 3: Health Benefits of Tai Chi

Though Tai chi began as an intense martial art (which some individuals are still practicing as that today), it has predominantly developed into more of a low-impact and aerobic form that is embraced by many to improve their physical and mental health. There are numerous claims of improved health which we can attribute to careful study and research.

1. **Enhanced Strength and Better Balance** – According to research conducted by the Oregon Research Institute, participants who have practiced tai chi were seen to have less difficulty in doing moderate to rigorous activities. The results were more evident in people who began in the poorest health. In other studies, tai chi exercises have been a contributor to the reduction of falls by elderly practitioners, and indeed, a fear of falling as well. The reason behind this is that the exercises have the ability to improve nerve sensitivity in knees and ankles, preventing falls in return.

2. **Improved Sleeping Patterns** – A recent study on tai chi states that it has a positive effect on sleeping patterns. People who practice Tai chi have been recorded as sleeping for longer. Perhaps more importantly, it has been known to improve sleep quality also. According to Chinese medicine, insomnia is caused by a disturbed spirit, which could be in a form of an unsettled mind. The best remedy for this is to harmonize the pathways of

the *qi* energy that is associated with consciousness of the mind and heart. Tai Chi is a great method for treating this issue, helping sleep-deprived people to gain back a more balanced life. It works by calming the nervous system and reducing the overactive mind, which can lead to a much better sleeping pattern.

3. **Better Walking Speed** – Walking speed is something that often reduces as we age. This may also be associated with the increased risk of falling, researchers have found. Those who practice Tai Chi, especially older people, are more likely to improve their walking speed and their confidence in doing so.

4. **Reduction of Stress** - Adults of all ages experience stress from time to time, be it at work or at home. Because of the relaxing movements, breathing patterns, and mental concentration involved in Tai chi, it can become a great source of distraction from a hectic lifestyle. Practicing Tai chi embraces peace and calmness as well as much greater mind-body coordination, reducing stress in the process.

5. **Aerobic Conditioning** – The ability to perform aerobic exercises also decreases with age. However, studies show that adults who incorporate Tai chi in their daily routines have a higher aerobic capacity than those of the same age who live a sedentary lifestyle. The benefits depend on the size of Tai chi movements and speed involved.

Medical Conditions: What Tai Chi Can Do

Aside from the potential health benefits of Tai chi, such as stress reduction and longer life, there are a number of symptoms present in medical conditions that can be alleviated by this mind-body practice. Numerous studies that have been conducted by medical researchers suggested this martial art form can not only enhance general health, but also combat disease.

Heart Disease

Patients with heart conditions who practice Tai chi are more likely to improve their quality of life and be more confident in performing physical activities. A study was conducted at National Taiwan University on 53 participants to determine the effects of Tai chi on a range of participants. Those who were in the Tai chi group showed significant improvements in triglycerides, cholesterol, C-reactive protein and insulin levels in people who were most likely to acquire heart disease. Blood pressure and aerobic capacity are often intrinsically related, and positive results in both areas were also noticed in those afflicted. On the other hand, participants who did not join Tai chi classes showed no improvement whatsoever.

Heart Failure

Patients with chronic systolic heart failure used to be considered too weak to exercise, thus in the past, they were not encouraged to engage in physical activities. Over the years, several studies have been conducted in connection to this. In one, Harvard Medical School enrolled 30 people for a pilot study and reported the positive effects of the practice on the participants in regards to their ability to walk. A reduction in B-type natriuretic protein blood levels, which is a red flag for heart failure, was also discovered.

Hypertension

Tai chi can also be used as an alternative modality in the management of hypertension. A review of 26 Chinese and English studies that can be read from Preventive Cardiology (Spring 2008) highlighted the ability of Tai chi to reduce blood pressure in 85% of the trials, showing improvements in systolic pressure from 3 to 32 mm Hg while a 2 to 18 mm hg reduction in diastolic pressure was also noted. Consequently, changes in lipid profile are seen as favorable.

Stroke

Individuals who have suffered from cerebrovascular accident (CVA), or what is commonly known as stroke, can speed up their recovery by incorporating Tai chi exercises in their therapy sessions and exercise routines. A study participated in by 136 patients who have suffered from stroke for a period of at least six months and was published in 2009 in the journal Neuro Rehabilitation and Neural Repair. Results showed improvement in balance and functionality of the patients after a 12-week Tai chi class. This improvement was greater than what patients who underwent traditional general exercise programs that included stretching, breathing and mobilizing the joints and muscles used for walking and sitting benefited from.

Arthritis

Tai chi is a safe alternative for elderly people for pain relief. Its gentle and fluid movements make Tai chi a natural workout for arthritis patients. In fact, major health organizations recommend the practice of Tai chi due to its ability to balance the mind and body as well as for it being low-impact in nature. A study conducted at Tufts University showed improvements in the physical functioning and moods of those participants who joined an hour of Tai chi class twice a week for a period of three months as opposed to patients suffering from severe knee osteoarthritis who use conventional exercise programs. A published Korean study reported the same results for people with ankylosing spondylitis, an inflammatory form of arthritis that affects the spine.

Breast Cancer

In a study at the University of Rochester, published in Medicine and Sport Science in 2008, breast cancer patients and those suffering from the side effects of breast cancer medications were able to go back to their normal routines of exercise and work after joining Tai chi classes for 12 weeks. Moreover, researchers saw significant improvements in the said patients in achieving functional capacity when it came to muscle strength, flexibility and aerobic capacity as well in self-esteem. On the other hand, those who were only having traditional supportive therapy did not experience the same level of results.

Low Bone Mineral Density

Postmenopausal women are prone to osteoporosis which is indicated by low bone mineral density (BMD). This bone disease is typified by decreased bone strength and is also associated with aging. Thus said, people who have low bone density are at risk for falling and fractures. By engaging in Tai chi, muscle strength and flexibility are improved as well as a person's sense of balance, making it highly recommend by medical practitioners. Tai chi is also considered to be a safe and effective way to maintain bone density in women who have reached postmenopausal age. A conducted study revealed that a 45-minute Tai chi session five times a week can slow down the rate of bone loss, 2.6 to 3.6 times of those women who were in the controlled group.

Parkinson's Disease

Patients with mild to moderate Parkinson's disease can also benefit from Tai chi. A gentle exercise program can improve balance and motor control in these patients. This was revealed by a pilot study published in Gait and Posture and conducted by researchers from Washington University School of Medicine. Participants included 33 individuals who have Parkinson's disease who were asked to participate in 20 sessions of Tai chi. After the given period, patients reported improvement in their walking ability, balance and overall wellness.

Sleep Problems

People who are having difficulty in sleeping, particularly the elderly, can also benefit from the practice of Tai chi. A study was conducted by the University of California to determine the effect of Tai chi on people who have mild cases of sleeplessness. Participants reported improvement in the quality of sleep compared to those who were given basic sleep education. This was published in the journal Sleep in June 2008.

As these researches have suggested, Tai chi, along with medications, can help patients suffering from certain medical conditions live more comfortably. It is, indeed, worth a try to get involved in Tai chi practices, even by just incorporating the easier styles into daily routines. The benefits of this exercise form are great, and one can never truly question its value to health. To expect more progress, it is crucial to consult your doctor before getting started.

Maintaining Its Health Benefits

A 12-week class schedule allows you to achieve the amazing benefits of Tai Chi. Recent studies also suggest that you will enjoy more of its benefits if you continue the practice for a longer time and master its elements.

You can practice it every day at the same time and in the same place to develop a routine. If you do happen to have a busy schedule, you can always practice for a few minutes whenever you can. Tai chi does not require you to be in class, as it can be done anywhere you like just as long as you are familiar with the movements, techniques, and postures of the Tai chi style you have chosen. You can also take the opportunity to introduce Tai chi's meditative practices to your friends and family members. In short, it does not require a whole lot of your time and a dedicated workout space to incorporate Tai chi into your daily routine.

Chapter 4: Getting Started with the Art of Tai Chi

Just like taking up any physical activity, engaging in the art of Tai chi entails preparation and effort. Attaining fluidity and smoothness in your movements does not happen in a day. As a beginner, it is best to start the right way. Here are some tips on getting started:

Visit a General Practitioner

Before starting any form of exercise program or physical activity, it is necessary to consult your doctor, especially those with medical conditions who are taking certain medications or are at risk of suffering from heart conditions. Tai chi, although reasonably safe compared with others, is not exempt from a recommendation to visit your GP before starting a routine. It is equally important to consider one's fitness levels. By visiting a health care professional, one can know which exercises are well within one's range of abilities. And with several studies showing the potential health benefits of Tai chi both mentally and physically, medical doctors are most likely to recommend this to patients.

Observe Tai Chi Classes and Consider Enlisting in One

With the continuing popularity of Tai chi in the United States and other parts of the Western world, signing up for a class in the community shouldn't be too difficult. Aside from local community centers, health clubs and martial arts studios are also great places to check out for Tai chi classes. The best way is firstly to observe and maybe ask for a trial session to get a feel for Tai chi. Watching the instructor in action and actually experiencing it first-hand makes it easier to decide if it will appeal to you. While at the studio, you can also get a sense of the environment and at the same time determine if the approach works for you. An instructor can also provide individual sessions at a given location or at home. In classes, several things will be learned like coordination, basic body alignments, the 70 percent rule of moderation, sequences of movements and how to protect the joints. But if you decide that you would like to begin your Tai chi journey at home, there are many instructional videos available on the market. Books are also available in stores and online for those who want to read and learn the basics of a 12-movement, easy-to-learn sequence from illustrations and photographs.

Know the Different Styles of Tai Chi and Choose What Works

For a beginner, the names of the various Tai chi styles and the level of complexity or simplicity of these movements can be quite confusing. Names such as Wu, Cheng, and Yang are the different styles with variations in the speed of movement and the way the body holds the postures. Some instructors will even encourage you to adopt a combination of the three styles. Also, there are programs where the martial arts aspect of Tai chi is given more emphasis than its health potential. While there are forms where one can learn long sequences of movements, there are other forms that focus on a series of short movements and involve meditation and breathing exercises. It is important to consider a low-pressure environment where you can learn at your own pace, and not exerting too much effort as to go beyond what is comfortable. Whichever your preferred style, it is best to commit to regular sessions, whether at home or at the gym, to so as to develop a rhythm of practice.

Find a Good Instructor

There are many Tai chi instructors ready to teach and guide those willing to learn. It isn't actually a requirement for standard licensing and training to teach Tai chi – the knowledge and ability to instruct is often the product of years of practice – but as such, it pays to do your research. Instructors' approaches will vary from one person to the next, and although their qualifications may not be brought into question, their methodology must certainly align with your own goals and preferences.

There are many resources to browse through on the internet. Centers of practice may well have their own websites and be listed in local directories, but it would be wise to seek the opinion of others who may have experience with your local options. Just as in any other area of life, word of mouth will often be your most valuable source of information.

A health care provider might also know instructors within the area. The key is to look for a teacher who can accommodate your health concerns and is able to adjust the program depending on your level of fitness and personal goals.

How Long Should I Commit to Tai Chi For?

It's an open question and one which will attract varying degrees of commitment. It is always best to take things slow, one step at a time, and simply judge how much you are enjoying it. You will no doubt experience some of the benefits immediately: increased flexibility, increase in energy levels, and the natural serotonin and endorphin rushes that come with any exercise program. But to start seeing truly recognizable health benefits, it pays to see your commitment to Tai chi endure over a number of weeks, months, or even years.

As medical research studies have shown, 12 weeks is a good starting point, although improvements appear to continue progressively the longer the practice continues.

Know that Tai Chi Can Be Challenging

Although Tai chi seems to be easy, given the fluidity and smoothness in the movements, learning this form of martial art can be a challenge. To be rightfully considered one of the most sophisticated methods of integrated whole body movement, one can reasonably expect to have to work to master the art. As with all aerobic exercises, it can be strenuous, but as your body adjusts to the new workload, you will notice a significant increase in fitness and stamina levels. Your Tai chi will that be much more enjoyable and you will naturally acquire the ability to push yourself further and further. It is important to give yourself enough time to do this though. Pushing yourself too hard too quickly could result in injury, and more importantly, a disdain for performing Tai chi.

Chapter 5: Tai Chi Basics: Weapons and Clothing

Although Tai chi can be performed in any manner of comfortable clothing styles, history and tradition often encourage practitioners to conform to wearing silk robes as its founders did all those years ago. If you are joining a class, you can expect to see more formal attire being worn, and advice on where to obtain some for yourself will surely be not far away. For participants of styles which require the use of weapons, a specialist martial arts center will be a good guide. The internet, in this instance, is probably not the best place to go shopping. But for beginners who are keen on putting tradition into practice, here are things you need to consider:

Clothing

Easy and comfortable—this is how the Tai chi clothing style is described by many. And this is how it should be. You can actually wear almost anything, as long as you consider the following questions: Can you perform the flowing movements of the art without being restricted by your clothing? Do you have the freedom to perform unique footwork without ripping the seams of your trousers?

- **Opt for the Traditional**

Traditional clothing includes silk robes or uniforms that were once worn by martial artists in ancient China. While there are a few Tai chi schools and clubs that still adopt what is traditional, most opt for a more comfortable and relaxing dress code. In tournaments or performances, advanced practitioners wear formal silks or uniforms.

- **Comfort Is Key**

To achieve the flow of *qi*, it is important to wear clothing that is comfortable and loose. Stretchy yoga pants, loose t-shirts, and athletic outfits are perfect for this type of workout. Not everybody wants to wear Tai chi uniforms, which is just fair because it solely depends on the participants' preference anyway.

- **Inspire Others**

If you are a beginner who wants to inspire fellow newcomers, you can dress to inspire others by donning silk robes. It is also a great way of creating a nice traditional atmosphere for a practice. Wearing what is appropriate for an event has a particular boosting effect, making the entire Tai chi session more beneficial for everyone.

- **Footwear Choices**

While there are people who practice barefoot, others can find this really difficult. A pair of shoes is often a must. Practice shoes should be flexible and comfortable. You will be performing light, quick-paced movements, so choose a pair that has proper support to help you balance. To minimize injury, shoes that have shock-absorbent pads in the sole are ideal.

Weapons

A good way to embrace the core of Tai chi is through the use of weapons. Usually introduced when practitioners have progressed in open-hand form, they vary in size, material, and weight. Weaponry forms in Tai chi exercises offer much that non-weapon based styles cannot. They are beautiful and interesting to both watch and perform. Moreover, the use of weapons requires movements that will improve your overall Tai chi skills. Here are several items that are suitable for those who want to include them in their practices:

- **Straight Sword**

It is usually straight with a double edge and weighs about 4-8 pounds. The purpose of the sword is to teach coordination between the body and the hand in terms of flexibility, fitness, and balance. To improve the flow through this weapon, the energy of the sword should be completely balanced. The best way to achieve so is through low stances and high one-legged postures. An equal amount of energy is expected from the opposite hand to allow more energy into the weapon.

- **Spear**

The spear is usually seven feet long with a head trimmed with horse hair and is made of wax wood. The use of this weapon is to extend energy outside of the body. It can be difficult to handle for beginners, but it offers an amassing power with constant practice.

- **Long Pole**

The long pole varies from 8 feet to 12 feet and is typically made of wood of the same thickness throughout the body. Wax wood is used in some styles, such as the Chen. The use of long poles allows practitioners to improve their stance and strengthen the spine.

As mentioned above, weapons are optional and their usage depends on your preference. Most beginners usually find handling a weapon a bit awkward during their first try. But just like Tai chi itself, it takes time to get used to the movements and feel the flow of energy within. Regular practice is key.

Chapter 6: Tai Chi Basic Moves for Beginners

The moves and techniques for Tai chi aim to reduce stress and improve health. They may sound extremely difficult, knowing that this art is for self-defense, but it is actually easy and can be done just about anywhere. Instructional DVDs and Tai chi schools and fitness centers teach these techniques.

Standing Meditation Technique

Considered as the most basic pose, the standing meditation technique is a vital aspect in the practice because it allows participants to find their ground or center both emotionally and physically. This, in turn, helps them discover the stillness within motion. The way to do this is as follows:

- Stand with your feet apart, toes pointing straight, and knees bent slightly.

- Keep shoulders relaxed and your head help up straight.

- Close your eyes and breathe slowly through your nose. Begin meditating.

- Imagine that you are pulling energy from the earth to your feet as you inhale. Likewise, return the said energy to the ground as you exhale.

- Repeat numerous times. Try to let the energy flow through your legs and up into the center of your body.

Windmill Exercise

To improve flexibility and open up the spine, the windmill exercise is the best form to practice. Here are the steps on how to do this:

- Stand with your shoulders relaxed, with your arms hung loosely and feet parallel and slightly apart.

- Place your hands in front of your body by your lap. Point your fingers toward the ground.

- Raise your arms up to the center of your body when you inhale, and slowly take your arms over your head with your fingers pointing upwards.

- Stretch and slowly bend your spine backwards.

- Exhale and bend forward, bringing your hands down to the center of the body.

- Bend further from your hip join and let your arms hang loosely.

- Inhale as you return to the starting pose.

Hand Exercises

The hand exercises involved in Tai chi promote flexibility in the shoulders, fingers, and arms. Try the following to attain the benefits of this form:

- Stand with your feet apart and slightly wider than your shoulder width.

- Bring your arms straight in front of you at shoulder level and parallel to the ground.

- Stretch as wide as you can. Rotate your wrists in a clockwise motion. Do this again, but in a counter-clockwise direction this time.

Knee Rolls

Knee rolls in Tai chi enhance mobility in the knees and spine. They also promote better balance. Achieve all benefits with these steps:

- Stand with your feet slightly apart and knees bent.

- Put your hands on your knees, letting your fingers point toward each other.

- Start rotating your knees as though you are tracing a big circle on the ground.

- Do so in a clockwise motion. Change directions after a few counts.

Closing Form

The closing posture is done at the end of the practice. This is to balance the energy and promote relaxation.

- Stand with relaxed shoulders and your feet slightly apart.

- Place your hands in front of your pelvis and in a cup position with the palms facing upwards.

- Inhale and exhale. Imagine that you are pulling and returning the energy from the ground to your body and vice versa. As you inhale, bring your hands to your chest.

- Slowly bring your palms to face the ground as you exhale.

The exercises above are easy and so basic that everyone can perform them without any difficulty. However, there are a few things that hinder some from starting an exercise regime. Procrastination and laziness are just some of the negative aspects that can pull your health down. They have to be removed from the mindset, otherwise, they can waste your energy on negative thinking. Control your mind and start incorporating these tips:

One Exercise at a Time

All of these exercises promote proper posture, better balance, and stronger joints. However, it can be hard for beginners to focus on a particular pose. The solution is to concentrate one principle at a time. What would you like to achieve? Which body aspect would you like to improve?

What you can do first is focus on the upper body, which includes the neck and the spine. The next time you do some basic steps, focus on the alignment of the hips or your breathing. And so on. This is the best way to see the improvements every time you practice Tai chi.

Patience

Tai chi involves slow, flowing moves, and it takes patience and concentration to make everything work. You might also find some poses difficult. Constant practice makes perfect. Do it regularly and all the elements of Tai chi will come together.

Embrace your limitations

Are you suffering from any medical conditions that restrict you from practicing Tai chi? Are you currently pregnant? Do you not believe your fitness levels are up to the challenge? Although Tai chi is generally safe, there are a few conditions that need to be considered. Before you start, embrace your limitations and know what you can do with them instead. Go to a medical practitioner and ask what types of Tai chi exercises are not only suitable for you, but actively improve that which you consider your weakest aspects.

To sum up, Tai chi is an old Chinese tradition that has become a beautiful form of exercise today. Its series of movements are performed in a slow and concentrated manner and are accompanied by deep and relaxing breathing. Because Tai chi puts minimal stress on joints and muscles, it is considered safe for all ages. Even older adults, who may not have participated in exercise for many years, should still find Tai chi a suitable and enjoyable pastime.

Conclusion

Thank you again for downloading this book!

I hope this book was able to help you to learn about the ancient martial art, Tai chi, and its plethora of benefits.

The next step upon successful completion of this book is to assess yourself and see if you are keen about advancing in Tai chi. In this book, we have laid everything there is to know about this martial art form for beginners, and you should be able to pinpoint which aspects apply to you best. Once you have mastered the art of Tai chi, great benefits await you, not only for your physical health but for the emotional and mental health as well.

Finally, if you enjoyed this book, please take the time to share your thoughts and post a review on Amazon. It'd be greatly appreciated!

Thank you and good luck!

Made in the USA
Coppell, TX
26 September 2021